CROW

Big Buddy Books
An Imprint of Abdo Publishing
abdopublishing.com

Katie Lajiness

abdopublishing.com

Published by Abdo Publishing, a division of ABDO, PO Box 398166, Minneapolis, Minnesota 55439.
Copyright © 2019 by Abdo Consulting Group, Inc. International copyrights reserved in all countries. No part
of this book may be reproduced in any form without written permission from the publisher. Big Buddy Books™
is a trademark and logo of Abdo Publishing.

Printed in the United States of America, North Mankato, Minnesota.
052018
092018

THIS BOOK CONTAINS
RECYCLED MATERIALS

Cover Photo: Marilyn Angel Wynn/Native Stock.
Background Photo: James Gabbert/Getty Images.
Interior Photos: Anna Kurzaeva/Getty Images (p. 11); Don Mammoser/Shutterstock (p. 23); Dorling Kindersley/Getty
    Images (p. 26); Edwin L. Wisherd/National Geographic Creative (pp. 5, 21); Jason O. Watson/Alamy Stock Photo
    (p. 19); Marilyn Angel Wynn/Native Stock (pp. 9, 13, 16, 17, 25, 29, 30); The Protected Art Archive/Alamy Stock
    Photo (p. 15); Tom Brakefield/Getty Images (p. 27).

Coordinating Series Editor: Tamara L. Britton
Graphic Design: Jenny Christensen, Maria Hosley

Library of Congress Control Number: 2017962678

Publisher's Cataloging-in-Publication Data

Name: Lajiness, Katie, author.
Title: Crow / by Katie Lajiness.
Description: Minneapolis, Minnesota : Abdo Publishing, 2019. | Series: Native Americans
    set 4 | Includes online resources and index.
Identifiers: ISBN 9781532115073 (lib.bdg.) | ISBN 9781532155796 (ebook)
Subjects: LCSH: Crow Indians--Juvenile literature. | Indians of North America--Juvenile
    literature. | Indigenous peoples--Social life and customs--Juvenile literature. |
    Cultural anthropology--Juvenile literature.
Classification: DDC 970.00497--dc23

CONTENTS

Amazing People

Hundreds of years ago, North America was mostly wild, open land. Native American tribes lived on the land. Each had its own language and special practices.

The Crow (KROH) are one Native American tribe. Many know them for their **ceremonies** and handmade crafts. Let's learn more about these Native Americans.

Did You Know?

The name *Crow* means "people of the crows."

There were two Crow groups, the Mountain and the River Crow. Each had its own chief.

CROW TERRITORY

The Crow tribe's early family members lived on the Great Plains for hundreds of years. Crow homelands were in what is now Wyoming and Montana. Since the 1800s, many Crow people have lived on **reservations** in Montana.

CANADA

UNITED STATES

CROW HOMELANDS

MONTANA

IDAHO

WYOMING

N
W   E
S

MEXICO

7

HOME LIFE

The Crow people lived in teepees. These could be quickly taken down as the tribe moved. The teepees were made with buffalo hides stretched over tree poles. Inside each teepee was a fire used to keep the inside warm. Smoke escaped from a hole at the top of the teepee.

Paintings decorated the outsides and insides of the teepees. Designs were original for each family.

WHAT THEY ATE

In the past, the Crow people mostly ate buffalo meat. They also hunted bighorn sheep, mountain goats, deer, elk, and bears. Sometimes, meat was roasted or boiled in a stew with root vegetables and herbs. Tribe members mixed dried meat with nuts and berries to make a trail food called pemmican.

Women gathered nuts, wild turnips, and berries for meals.

Daily Life

Crow men and women wore different styles of clothes. But they all had long hair. The Crow used grease to make their hair shiny.

Women wore deer or buffalo-skin dresses. Everyone had warm leggings and moccasins. Their clothes were decorated using elk teeth or shells. And tribe members often wore fur robes in the winter.

The Crow people created beautiful beadwork. They added beads to robes, vests, pants, and moccasins.

Crow women prepared food, took care of the home, and made clothes. They also took care of the children. Men hunted animals and protected the tribes.

Men often attacked villages to steal horses. Later, the tribe used or sold the horses.

MADE BY HAND

The Crow made many objects by hand. They often used natural supplies. These arts and crafts added beauty to everyday life.

Sweet Grass
Women braided green grass. Then they dried the grass and lit it with fire during ceremonies.

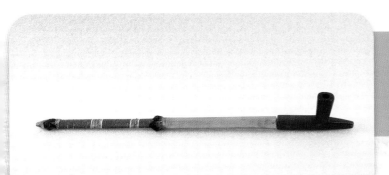

Stem Pipe
Men smoked pipes made with colorful wooden stems. Women painted the stems using porcupine quills.

Medicine Bag
Women added beads to leather medicine bags.

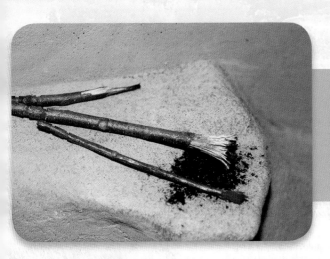

Paintbrushes
Paintbrushes were made from small sticks that were soft at one end.

SPIRIT LIFE

The **vision** quest was a part of the Crow tribe's spirit life. Those seeking a vision prayed and **fasted** for days. Then, a spiritual guide visited the seeker in a vision. When the seeker gained power, he shared it with other men in the tribe.

Crowheart Butte in Wyoming is a holy place for many Crow people. Only Native Americans are allowed to climb it.

Storytellers

Stories were important to the Crow. Older tribe members told stories for fun and to teach lessons.

Like most other tribes, the Crow also had a creation story. The Creator asked four ducks to bring mud up from the bottom of a lake. The first three ducks failed, but the fourth brought up some mud. The Crow people were created from this mud.

Crow families gathered together to tell stories. These tales helped keep their history alive.

21

Fighting for Land

For 200 years, Europeans and enemy tribes arrived in large numbers. They fought the Crow for control of hunting lands. But the Crow did not want **violence**. So, they became friends with the settlers.

A monument at Little Bighorn Battlefield National Park honors those lost in battle.

Even after signing many **treaties**, the Crow still lost their land. In 1851, the US government began a Crow **reservation**. The tribe accepted a smaller piece of land in Montana in 1868. Finally, the Crow settled on their current reservation at Crow Agency in Montana.

The Crow Fair is near Billings, Montana. More than 1,000 teepees are open for people to stay in.

BACK IN TIME

1600s

The Hidatsa tribe separated into two different groups. One of those groups was the Crow tribe.

1400s

Early Crow family members lived on the Great Plains.

1700s

The Crow found their first horses at a Shoshone camp in Utah.

1805

Explorers Meriwether Lewis and William Clark traveled across the Crow's land.

1888

Crow Chief Two Leggings led an attack against a Lakota group. This was the last battle between native tribes in the northern Great Plains.

1914

Crow men served in **World War I**.

1987

The Supreme Court gave millions of dollars to the Crow Nation. This was payment for land stolen from the tribe in the 1800s.

2002

The Crow tribe passed a new **constitution**. This allowed the tribe to have its own laws.

THE CROW TODAY

The Crow have a long, rich history. Many remember them for their beautiful beadwork.

Crow roots run deep. Today, the people have held on to those special things that make them Crow. Even though times have changed, many people carry the **traditions**, stories, and memories of the past into the present.

Did You Know?

Today, about 10,000 members live on or near the Montana reservation.

The Crow continue to pass their traditions down to young children.

"We may not know what may happen today, but let us act as though we were the Seven Stars [Big Dipper] in the sky that live forever. Go with me as far as you can, and I will go with you while there is breath in my body."

— Chief Plenty Coups, Crow

GLOSSARY

ceremony a formal event on a special occasion.

constitution (kahnt-stuh-TOO-shuhn) the basic laws that govern a country or a state.

explorer a person who travels to new or unknown places.

fast to go without eating food.

medicine (MEH-duh-suhn) an item used in or on the body to treat an illness, ease pain, or heal a wound.

reservation (reh-zuhr-VAY-shuhn) a piece of land set aside by the government for Native Americans to live on.

tradition (truh-DIH-shuhn) a belief, a custom, or a story handed down from older people to younger people.

treaty an agreement made between two or more groups.

violence the use of force to harm a person or damage property.

vision something dreamed or imagined.

World War I a war fought in Europe from 1914 to 1918.

Online Resources

Booklinks
NONFICTION NETWORK
FREE! ONLINE NONFICTION RESOURCES

To learn more about the Crow, visit **abdobooklinks.com**. These links are routinely monitored and updated to provide the most current information available.

INDEX